# donna hay

SIMPLE ESSENTIALS

# chocolate

## thank you

Putting together a book is like doing one big jigsaw puzzle. When you begin there are ideas scattered here, concepts scattered there. Then it all starts to take shape and what once seemed impossible suddenly becomes reality. For helping to complete the final (beautiful!) picture I have so many people to thank: Vanessa Pitsikas, for being a designer wise, composed and talented beyond her years; recipe tester Jane Collings for dishes that elicit oohs and aahs every time; superlative copy editor Kirsty McKenzie for always asking the right questions; the amazing Con Poulos, talented Chris Court and all the other photographers whose images shine on every page; and, of course, to the *donna hay magazine* staff for being all-round superstars – your loyalty, creativity and professionalism help make donna hay a truly world-class brand. Many thanks must also be extended to Phil Barker and Peter Byrne at News Magazines; and to the team at HarperCollins. Thank you, thank you, thank you to friends old and new and my dear family. And to the men in my life: my extraordinary sons Angus and Tom who make my heart soar, and my partner Bill.

### on the cover

front: molten chocolate puddings, page 76
back: melt-and-mix chocolate coconut cake, page 58

### Ecco

An imprint of HarperCollins*Publishers*

First American edition published 2008
First Australian edition published 2007
HarperCollins*Publishers*,
25 Ryde Road, Pymble, Sydney, NSW 2073, Australia
77-85 Fulham Palace Road, London W6 8JB, United Kingdom
2 Bloor Street East, 20th Floor, Toronto, Ontario M4W1A8, Canada
31 View Road, Glenfield, Auckland 10, New Zealand
10 East 53rd Street, New York, NY 10022, USA

Designer: Vanessa Pitsikas
Copy Editor: Kirsty McKenzie
Food Editors: Justine Poole, Steve Pearce, Jane Collings
Consulting Editor: Jana Frawley
Consulting Art Director: Sarah Kavanagh

Reproduction by Graphic Print Group, South Australia
Produced in Hong Kong by Phoenix Offset on 157gsm Chinese Matt Art.
Printed in China.

Library of Congress Cataloging-in-Publication Data has been applied for.

ISBN-13: 978-0-06-156902-9

First Ecco Edition 2008
08 09 10 11 /IMP 10 9 8 7 6 5 4 3 2 1

# donna hay

SIMPLE ESSENTIALS

# chocolate

**ecco**

An Imprint of HarperCollins*Publishers*

# contents

## introduction

While chocolate may not exactly be able to solve all the
world's problems, I firmly believe that large quantities of
the almost mythological substance that comes from the
cacao bean could have a profound impact on many a dicey
international situation. The sharing of chocolate is an act
of love. The generosity of the gesture brings smiles to
faces, lifts spirits and restores good humour. Just about
everyone I know is a confirmed chocoholic and when
there's chocolate around it's destined for a short shelf life.
We've trawled through everyone's personal favourite
recipes to bring together the best ever collection of
chocolate treats. Indulge and do your bit for world peace.

Donna

# basics

Cooking with chocolate can seem a bit tricky at the outset but if you have a brief understanding of the basics, you'll sail through like a pro. Our simple instructions guide you through the different chocolate varieties, when to use them and how to achieve perfect results every time. You'll be melting chocolate without a qualm and whipping up glazes, icings and desserts like you've been doing it all your life.

# all about chocolate

Chocolate is made by extracting cocoa solids and cocoa butter
from roasted cacao beans and blending them in varying quantities.
Solids provide rich, bitter flavour and butter, the smooth mouth-feel.

## couverture

Couverture is French for "covering" and this
is the chocolate professionals generally
use for dipping and glazing. It has a higher
percentage of cocoa butter than ordinary
chocolate which means it is glossier and
has more flavour which of course carries
through to the finished recipe. Couvertures
with varying amounts of cocoa solids
(ranging from 30–85 per cent) are
available from cooking stores and delis.
Dark chocolate contains 54–57 per cent
cocoa solids. More bitter couverture has
64 per cent or higher cocoa solids.

## milk chocolate

The most popular eating chocolate
around, milk chocolate generally has
fewer cocoa solids and more sugar than
cooking varieties. As the name suggests,
milk chocolate contains milk powder
or condensed milk. Like most chocolate
it will keep for up to a year if stored
tightly wrapped in a dry, dark spot at
around 21°C (70°F).

## white chocolate

Most white chocolate doesn't contain
cocoa solids and therefore isn't technically
chocolate. It is made from cocoa butter,
sugar, milk and vanilla. Products that
contain higher proportions of vegetable
oils instead of cocoa butter won't have
the depth of flavour of quality white
chocolate. So check the label for the list
of ingredients before you buy. You may
need to go to a cooking store to buy white
chocolate with low vegetable oil content.

## compound chocolate

When cooking with chocolate remember
the better the quality, the better the result.
Compound chocolate, in which some of
the cocoa butter is replaced by vegetable
oil, does not have the flavour and texture
of the more expensive chocolates, but it is
easy to work with because it melts quickly
and is more forgiving than other varieties.

## chocolate melts

Also known as chocolate buttons, melts
are made from compound chocolate and
are available in white, milk and dark
varieties. Because of the higher vegetable
oil content the melted buttons don't set
as quickly as higher quality chocolate.
This makes them ideal for piping.

## chocolate bits

Destined for use in chocolate chip cookies
and muffins, chocolate bits or chips often
have less cocoa butter than bar chocolate,
which helps them retain their shape when
they're baked. Avoid chips that contain
high proportions of vegetable oil instead
of cocoa butter as they can have a waxy
taste. You can substitute roughly chopped
compound or couverture.

# all about chocolate

## origins

The South Americans and Mexicans introduced chocolate to the Spanish conquistadors in the 15th century and they in turn took the bewitching beverage back to Europe. Chocolate remained best known as a drink until the early 19th century, when English confectioners Fry's manufactured the first bars. Recently single origin varieties from Indonesia, Africa and South America have become popular for their distinctive characters.

## cocoa powder

Cocoa powder is made by rolling cocoa solids to produce a dark, bitter powder which is used in cooking and as a base for drinks. Choose an acidic (natural) or good-quality processed alkalised Dutch cocoa powder (available from speciality cooking shops and delicatessens) for good flavour and results. Dutch cocoa has a more delicate flavour than the robust, bitter natural cocoa powder which imparts a deeper chocolate flavour.

# how to melt

## stove top

Chocolate is quite fragile to cook with as it burns easily. Properly melted chocolate should be glossy and smooth. Melt chocolate in a dry heatproof bowl over simmering water, but don't let the bowl touch the water or the chocolate will burn, and don't let any water in the bowl or the chocolate will "seize" and become grainy. Stir occasionally until the chocolate is smooth. Only place chocolate over direct heat when another ingredient, such as cream, has been added to it.

## microwave

Short bursts is the secret to successfully melting chocolate in the microwave. Chop the chocolate and place it in a microwave safe container. Heat the chocolate in the microwave on the medium/low setting in 1 minute bursts, stirring after each time. When the chocolate seems two-thirds melted, stir to melt the remaining chocolate as microwaves keep cooking after the bowl has been removed from the microwave oven.

## tempering chocolate

Tempering is the process of heating and cooling chocolate to crystallise or solidify the cocoa butter to produce a smooth, glossy finish for dipping and glazing. If not tempered properly chocolate can look dull and streaky. You'll need a sugar (candy) thermometer to temper chocolate successfully. Melt two-thirds of the chocolate over hot water to 45°C (113°F). Stir in remaining chocolate until melted and the temperature will drop rapidly, then reheat to 30°C (86°F) when the chocolate should be easy to work with.

# chocolate essentials

## basic chocolate icing

Place 2 cups (300g/10½ oz) sifted icing (confectioner's) sugar
in a bowl with ⅓ cup (40g/1½ oz) sifted cocoa powder and
2 tablespoons boiling water. Stir until smooth. Spread icing over
a chilled cake. A chilled cake holds the icing on the cake and it
also allows you to make perfect drips down the side of the cake.

## chocolate glaze

Place 150g (5 oz) chopped dark couverture chocolate and
½ cup (125ml/4 fl oz) (single or pouring) cream in a small
saucepan over low heat, stirring until melted and smooth.
Allow the mixture to stand for 10 minutes and to thicken slightly.
Pour the glaze over a well chilled cake and tap to remove any
air bubbles. Or refrigerate the glaze and serve it as a rich
chocolate sauce with desserts.

## chocolate fudge icing

Place 250g (8 oz) dark couverture chocolate, ½ cup (125ml/4 fl oz) (single or pouring) cream and 70g (2½ oz) butter in a heatproof bowl over a saucepan of simmering water. Stir until melted and smooth. Remove and set aside to cool completely then beat with electric beaters until thick and fluffy. Spread over a chilled cake. To make white chocolate fudge icing substitute 250g (8 oz) white chocolate for the dark couverture.

## chocolate ganache

Place 1½ cups (375ml/12 fl oz) (single or pouring) cream in a saucepan over medium heat and bring to the boil. Remove from heat and add 340g (12 oz) finely chopped dark chocolate. Allow to melt slightly and then stir until glossy and smooth. Set aside to cool. Spread over a chilled cake or between layers of cake. Or roll into balls to make truffles.

# *chocolate essentials*

## hot chocolate fudge sauce

Place 200g (7 oz) chopped dark chocolate, ½ cup (125ml/ 4 fl oz) (single or pouring) cream, 2 tablespoons honey and 50g (1¾ oz) butter in a small saucepan over low heat and stir for 4–5 minutes or until the mixture is melted and smooth. Serve immediately. Makes 1½ cups (375ml/12 fl oz). Pour hot chocolate fudge sauce over ice-cream and cakes.

## hot chocolate

If you're going to make it yourself, you might as well have the best, so it's important to use high-quality chocolate. Heat 1 cup (250ml/8 fl oz) milk per person in a small saucepan until it's warmed through and close to boiling. Then add 1 tablespoon grated chocolate for each serving to the saucepan. If you're making for one, you can pour the hot milk directly onto the chocolate in a cup and stir. Serve with marshmallows if desired.

## chocolate mousse

Melt 200g (7 oz) chocolate and 75g (2¾ oz) butter in a small
saucepan over low heat and stir until smooth. Pour into a bowl
and beat in 4 egg yolks, one at a time. Set aside. Whip 1 cup
(250ml/8 fl oz) (single or pouring) cream to soft peaks. Set aside.
Whisk 4 egg whites to soft peaks. Whisk in 2 tablespoons icing
(confectioner's) sugar until thick and glossy. Fold cream into
chocolate, then egg whites. Refrigerate for 3 hours. Serves 6.

## basic chocolate custard

Place 2¼ cups (560ml/18 fl oz) (single or pouring) cream and
60g (2 oz) chopped dark chocolate in a saucepan over low
heat, stir until smooth, then bring to the boil. Set aside. Place
4 egg yolks, ¼ cup (55g/1⅞ oz) caster (superfine) sugar and
1 tablespoon cornflour (cornstarch) in a bowl, whisk to combine.
Pour cream mixture over the egg, whisking well. Return to pan
and stir over low heat for 1–2 minutes or until custard thickens.

# biscuits + slices

Everyone will want a slice of the action when the cookie jar is opened to reveal this assortment of biscuits and slices. Simple, time-honoured favourites and updates on the classics share the common denominators of an irresistible chocolate hit and good keepability. That's assuming you keep the location a secret. Once revealed, this selection is bound for a short, but sweet, life.

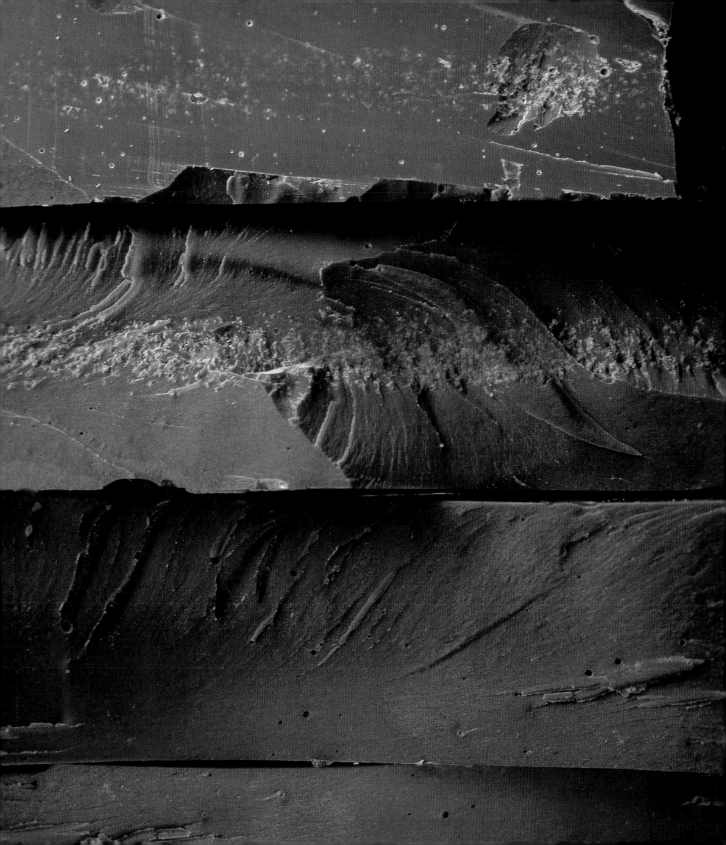

double chocolate cookies

white chocolate and macadamia cookies

raspberry-spiked chocolate brownies

## double chocolate cookies

110g (3½ oz) unsalted butter, softened
¾ cup (130g/4½ oz) brown sugar
1 egg
1 teaspoon vanilla extract
1 cup (150g/5¼ oz) plain (all-purpose) flour, sifted
¼ cup (30g/1 oz) cocoa powder, sifted
1 teaspoon bicarbonate of soda (baking soda)
125g (4 oz) dark chocolate, melted
280g (9¾ oz) dark chocolate, extra, roughly chopped

Preheat the oven to 160°C (320°F). Place the butter and sugar in the
bowl of an electric mixer and beat for 8−10 minutes or until light and
creamy. Add the egg and vanilla and beat for a further 3−4 minutes.
Stir through the flour, cocoa, bicarbonate of soda and melted chocolate.
Add the extra chopped chocolate and stir to combine. Roll tablespoons
of the mixture into rounds. Place on baking trays lined with non-stick
baking paper, allowing room for the cookies to spread, and flatten
slightly. Bake for 10−12 minutes or until slight cracks have formed.
Cool on wire racks. Makes 16.

## white chocolate and macadamia cookies

125g (4 oz) butter, softened
½ teaspoon vanilla extract
1 cup (220g/7¾ oz) caster (superfine) sugar
1 egg
1 cup (150g/5¼ oz) plain (all-purpose) flour, sifted
1 cup (150g/5¼ oz) self-raising (self-rising) flour, sifted
1 cup chopped unsalted macadamia nuts
250g (8 oz) white chocolate, chopped

Preheat the oven to 180°C (350°F). Place the butter, vanilla and sugar
in the bowl of an electric mixer and beat until light and creamy.
Add the egg and beat well. Add the flours, nuts and chocolate and
beat until combined. Roll 2 tablespoons of the mixture at a time into
balls, place the balls on baking trays lined with non-stick baking paper
and flatten slightly. Bake for 12 minutes or until cookies are lightly
browned. Cool on trays. Makes 22.

## raspberry-spiked chocolate brownies

200g (7 oz) dark chocolate, chopped
250g (8 oz) butter
1¾ cups (205g/7¼ oz) brown sugar
4 eggs
1⅓ cups (200g/7 oz) plain (all-purpose) flour
¼ teaspoon baking powder
⅓ cup (40g/1½ oz) cocoa powder, sifted
1½ cups raspberries, fresh or frozen+

Preheat the oven to 180°C (350°F). Place the chocolate and butter
in a small saucepan over low heat and stir until melted and smooth.
Place in a bowl with the sugar and eggs. Sift over the flour, baking
powder and cocoa and mix to combine. Pour into a 23cm (9 in)
greased square cake tin lined with non-stick baking paper. Top the
mixture with the raspberries and bake for 45 minutes or until set.
Brownies should be very fudgey in middle. Makes 16.
+ You can also use fresh or frozen blueberries. If using frozen berries
there is no need to defrost them first.

## chocolate crunch slice

⅓ cup (80ml/ 2½ fl oz) (single or pouring) cream
450g (15¾ oz) dark chocolate, chopped
130g (4½ oz) butter, chopped
250g (8 oz) store-bought shortbread biscuits, chopped
cocoa powder, for dusting

Place the cream, chocolate and butter in a saucepan over low heat
and stir until melted and combined. Place biscuits in a mixing bowl
and pour over two-thirds of the chocolate mixture, and stir to coat.
Spoon into a 32 x 7 x 8cm (12½ x 2¾ x 3 in) bar tin lined with
non-stick baking paper. Pour remaining chocolate mixture over and
tap tin to remove bubbles. Refrigerate for 3 hours or until set. To serve,
remove from tin, dust with cocoa and cut into slices. Makes 16.

chocolate crunch slice

chocolate and hazelnut cookies                    chocolate brownies

choc-studded honey wafers

## chocolate and hazelnut cookies

250g (8 oz) butter, softened
1 cup (175g/6 oz) brown sugar
¾ cup (165g/5¾ oz) sugar
3 eggs
2½ cups (450g/15¾ oz) plain (all-purpose) flour, sifted
½ cup (60g/2 oz) cocoa powder, sifted
1 teaspoon baking powder
*chocolate hazelnut filling*
150g (5 oz) dark chocolate
¾ cup (190g/6¾ oz) sour cream
1 cup hazelnuts, roasted and chopped

Preheat the oven to 150°C (300°F). Place the butter, brown sugar and sugar in a bowl and beat until light and creamy. Add the eggs gradually and beat well. Add the flour, cocoa and baking powder and mix until combined. Roll tablespoons of the mixture into balls, place on baking trays lined with non-stick baking paper and flatten slightly. Bake for 15 minutes or until bases are lightly coloured. Cool on racks.

To make the chocolate filling, melt the chocolate in a heatproof bowl over simmering water. Remove from the heat, add the sour cream and stir to combine. Top half of the biscuits with chocolate hazelnut filling and sprinkle with the nuts, top with the remaining biscuits. Makes 28.

## chocolate brownies

200g (7 oz) dark couverture (basics, page 10), chopped
250g (8 oz) butter, chopped
1¾ cups (205g/7¼ oz) brown sugar
4 eggs
⅓ cup (40g/1½ oz) cocoa powder, sifted
1 cup (150g/5¼ oz) plain (all-purpose) flour, sifted
¼ teaspoon baking powder

Preheat the oven to 160°C (320°F). Place the chocolate and butter in a saucepan over low heat and stir until smooth. Allow to cool slightly. Place the sugar, eggs, cocoa, flour and baking powder in a bowl. Add the chocolate mixture and mix until combined. Pour the mixture into a 23cm (9 in) square tin lined with non-stick baking paper. Bake for 30–35 minutes or until set. Cool in the tin. Cut into 16 slices.

## choc-studded honey wafers

50g (1¾ oz) butter, chopped
2 tablespoons honey
⅓ cup (60g/2 oz) brown sugar
⅓ cup (50g/1¾ oz) plain (all-purpose) flour, sifted
½ teaspoon vanilla extract
2 egg whites
½ cup blanched almonds, roasted and chopped
½ cup dark chocolate, chopped

Preheat the oven to 180°C (350°F). Place the butter and honey in a small saucepan over low heat until melted. Place the sugar, flour, vanilla and egg whites in a bowl, add the butter mixture and whisk until smooth. Place 2 teaspoonfuls of the mixture onto a baking tray lined with non-stick baking paper. Spread out to a 10cm (4 in) circle and sprinkle with the nuts and chocolate. Repeat with the remaining mixture. Bake for 8–10 minutes or until golden. Makes 24.

## triple chocolate skillet cookie

125g (4 oz) butter, softened
¾ cup (165g/5¾ oz) caster (superfine) sugar
½ teaspoon vanilla extract
1 egg
1¼ cups (190g/6¾ oz) plain (all-purpose) flour
¼ cup (30g/1 oz) cocoa powder
¼ cup chopped roasted hazelnuts
½ cup chopped milk chocolate
½ cup chopped white chocolate

Preheat the oven to 180°C (350°F). Place butter, sugar and vanilla in the bowl of an electric mixer and beat until light and creamy. Add the egg and beat well. Sift the flour and cocoa over and fold through with nuts and chocolate. Press dough into a lightly greased 19cm (7½ in) flat, ovenproof frying pan. Bake for 35 minutes, or until cooked through. Cool in the pan and cut into wedges. Serves 4–6.

triple chocolate skillet cookie

## chocolate-filled biscuits

65g (2¼ oz) cold butter, chopped
¼ cup (40g/1½ oz) icing (confectioner's) sugar
½ cup (75g/2½ oz) plain (all-purpose) flour
2½ teaspoons cornflour (cornstarch)
1 tablespoon cocoa powder
1 egg yolk
½ quantity chocolate ganache (recipe, page 15)

Preheat the oven to 180°C (350°F). Process the butter, icing sugar, flour, cornflour, cocoa and egg yolk in a food processor until a soft dough forms. Wrap in plastic wrap and refrigerate for 30 minutes. Roll teaspoonfuls of the mixture into balls, place on baking trays lined with non-stick baking paper and flatten slightly. Bake for 5–7 minutes or until the bases are lightly cooked. Cool on trays. Sandwich the biscuits with chocolate ganache. Makes 22.

## white chocolate panforte

¾ cup (165g/5¾ oz) caster (superfine) sugar
1 cup (250ml/8 fl oz) honey
1 cup unsalted macadamia nuts
1 cup unsalted cashew nuts
1 cup chopped dried apricots
1¼ cups (190g/6¾ oz) plain (all-purpose) flour
360g (12½ oz) white chocolate, melted
¼ teaspoon mixed spice
icing (confectioner's) sugar, for dusting

Preheat the oven to 160°C (320°F). Place the sugar and honey in a small saucepan over low heat and stir until the sugar has dissolved. Place the macadamias, cashews, apricots and flour in a bowl, add the honey mixture, chocolate and mixed spice and stir well to combine. Press into a greased and non-stick baking paper lined 22cm (8½ in) round springform tin and smooth the top with the back of a spoon. Bake for 25 minutes or until the top is golden. (It will still feel soft but will set as it cools.) Cool the panforte in the tin. Slice and dust with icing sugar. Serves 6–8.

chocolate-filled biscuits

white chocolate panforte

blondie                              panforte

chocolate caramel slice

## blondie

180g (6 oz) white chocolate
125g (4 oz) butter
1¾ cups (385g/13½ oz) caster (superfine) sugar
1 teaspoon vanilla extract
4 eggs
1⅔ cups (250g/8 oz) plain (all-purpose) flour
¼ teaspoon baking powder

Preheat the oven to 160°C (320°F). Place the chocolate and butter in a small saucepan over low heat and stir until melted and smooth. Place in a bowl with the sugar, vanilla and eggs. Sift over flour and baking powder and mix to combine. Pour the mixture into a 22cm (8½ in) square cake tin lined with non-stick baking paper. Bake for 1 hour or until set. Cut into slices. Makes 16.

## panforte

1 cup toasted almonds, roughly chopped
¾ cup roasted hazelnuts, roughly chopped
1 cup chopped dried apricots
1½ cups (225g/7⅞ oz) plain (all-purpose) flour, sifted
¼ cup (30g/1 oz) cocoa powder, sifted
1 teaspoon cinnamon
¼ teaspoon allspice
1 cup (250ml/8 fl oz) honey
1 cup (220g/7¾ oz) caster (superfine) sugar
rice paper, for lining (see glossary)

Preheat the oven to 180°C (350°F). Place the nuts, apricots, flour, cocoa, cinnamon and allspice in a large heatproof bowl. Place the honey and sugar in a saucepan and stir over a low heat until the sugar is dissolved. Brush the sides of the pan with a pastry brush dipped in water to remove any sugar crystals. Increase the heat and simmer for 1–2 minutes until "soft ball" stage (113–115°C/235–240°F) (use a sugar or candy thermometer (see glossary). Pour into the flour mixture and stir quickly to combine. Line a 20 x 30cm (8 x 12 in) slice tin with sheets of rice paper and trim the edges. Press the mixture into the tin. Cook for 20 minutes or until springy. Cool in the tin. Cut into slices. Makes 24.

## chocolate caramel slice

1 cup (150g/5¼ oz) plain (all-purpose) flour
½ cup (40g/1½ oz) desiccated coconut
½ cup (90g/3 oz) brown sugar
125g (4 oz) butter, melted
*caramel filling*
⅓ cup (2½ fl oz) golden syrup
125g (4 oz) butter, melted
2 x 400g (14 oz) cans sweetened condensed milk
1 quantity chocolate topping (recipe, page 88)

Preheat the oven to 180°C (350°F). Place the flour, coconut, sugar and butter in a bowl and mix well. Press the mixture into a 20 x 30cm (8 x 12 in) slice tin lined with non-stick baking paper and bake for 15–18 minutes or until brown.

To make the caramel filling, place the golden syrup, butter and condensed milk in a saucepan over low heat and stir for 7 minutes or until the caramel has thickened slightly. Pour over the cooked base and bake for 20 minutes or until the caramel is golden. Refrigerate the slice until cold. Spread with chocolate topping. Makes 30.

## chocolate and almond biscotti

1¾ cups (270g/9½ oz) plain (all-purpose) flour, sifted
1½ teaspoons baking powder
¼ cup (30g/1 oz) cocoa powder, sifted
¾ cup (165g/5¾ oz) caster (superfine) sugar
¾ cup blanched almonds
3 eggs
2½ teaspoons vanilla extract

Preheat the oven to 160°C (320°F). Place the flour, baking powder, cocoa, sugar and almonds in a bowl and mix together. Add the eggs and vanilla and mix well to form a dough. Divide the dough in two. Place the dough on a lightly floured surface and knead each piece until smooth. Shape into logs and flatten slightly. Place the logs on a baking tray lined with non-stick baking paper and bake for 35 minutes. Remove from oven and allow to cool completely. Cut logs into slices 5mm (¼ in) thick and place on baking trays lined with non-stick baking paper. Bake for 25 minutes or until biscotti are crisp. Makes 40.

chocolate and almond biscotti

## chocolate chip cookies

125g (4 oz) butter, softened
½ teaspoon vanilla extract
1 cup (175g/6 oz) brown sugar
2 eggs
2 cups (300g/10½ oz) plain (all-purpose) flour, sifted
1 teaspoon baking powder
1 cup (75g/2½ oz) desiccated coconut
185g (6½ oz) milk or dark chocolate, broken into small chunks

Preheat the oven to 190°C (375°C). Place the butter, vanilla and sugar in a bowl and beat until creamy. Beat in the eggs. Stir through the flour, baking powder, coconut and chocolate. Roll tablespoonfuls of the mixture into balls. Place on baking trays lined with non-stick baking paper, allowing room for the cookies to spread, and flatten slightly. Bake for 10–12 minutes or until lightly browned. Makes 38.

## chocolate cheesecake brownie

185g (6½ oz) butter, melted
¼ cup (30g/1 oz) cocoa powder, sifted
1 cup (220g/7¾ oz) caster (superfine) sugar
2 eggs
1 cup (150g/5¼ oz) plain (all-purpose) flour, sifted
*cheesecake*
285g (10 oz) cream cheese, softened and chopped
4½ tablespoons caster (superfine) sugar
2 eggs

Preheat the oven to 160°C (320°F). Place the butter, cocoa, sugar, eggs and flour in a bowl and mix well until smooth. Spoon into a 20cm (8 in) square slice tin lined with non-stick baking paper.

To make the cheesecake, process the cream cheese, sugar and eggs in a food processor until smooth. Place large spoonfuls of the cheesecake mixture on top of the chocolate mixture and swirl with a butter knife. Bake for 45–50 minutes or until set. Cool in the tin. Cut into 16 slices.

chocolate chip cookies

chocolate cheesecake brownie

# small cakes

Good things, they say, come in small packages. Especially when that package is a petite piece of perfection in the form of a cupcake, friand, muffin, bun or tart. Dress them up with fruit, cream or ice-cream and you have fuss-free, prepare-ahead desserts. Or keep it simple and serve with tea or coffee for morning or afternoon tea, a late night snack… or indeed, any time the mood strikes for a chocolate-laden sweet sensation.

chocolate friands

white chocolate cupcakes                    milk chocolate chunk muffins

## chocolate friands

1 cup (110g/3¾ oz) almond meal
1⅔ cups (250g/8 oz) icing (confectioner's) sugar, sifted
½ cup (75g/2½ oz) plain (all-purpose) flour, sifted
¼ cup (30g/1 oz) cocoa powder, sifted
½ teaspoon baking powder
5 egg whites
200g (7 oz) butter, melted

Preheat the oven to 160°C (320°F). Place the almond meal, icing sugar, flour, cocoa and baking powder in a bowl and stir to combine. Add the egg whites and stir to combine. Add the butter and stir to combine. Grease 12 x ½ cup (125ml/4 fl oz) capacity oval muffin tins. Spoon the mixture into tins and bake for 15–20 minutes or until springy to the touch. Makes 12.

## white chocolate cupcakes

100g (3½ oz) butter, softened
¾ cup (165g/5¾ oz) caster (superfine) sugar
2 eggs
1⅓ cups (200g/7 oz) plain (all-purpose) flour
1 teaspoon baking powder
½ cup (125ml/4 fl oz) milk
100g (3½ oz) white chocolate, melted
1 quantity white chocolate fudge icing (recipe, page 14)
fresh blueberries and icing (confectioner's) sugar, to serve

Preheat the oven to 160°C (320°F). Place the butter and sugar in the bowl of an electric mixer and beat until light and creamy. Gradually add eggs and beat well. Sift over flour and baking powder and beat until combined. Fold through the milk and chocolate, and spoon the mixture into 12 x ½ cup (125ml/4 fl oz) capacity muffin tins lined with paper patty cases. Bake for 20–25 minutes, or until cooked when tested with a skewer. Cool on wire racks. Spread white chocolate fudge icing over cupcakes, top with blueberries and dust with icing sugar, if desired. Makes 12.

## milk chocolate chunk muffins

2 cups (300g/10½ oz) self-raising (self-rising) flour, sifted
⅓ cup (40g/1½ oz) cocoa powder, sifted
1 teaspoon baking powder
1 cup (220g/7¾ oz) caster (superfine) sugar
2 eggs
1 teaspoon vanilla extract
⅔ cup (160ml/5 fl oz) vegetable oil
½ cup (125ml/4 fl oz) milk
1 cup chopped milk chocolate

Preheat the oven to 180°C (350°F). Place the flour, cocoa, baking powder and sugar into a bowl and mix to combine. In a separate bowl, combine the eggs, vanilla, oil and milk and whisk together. Stir the egg mixture into the flour mixture until just combined. Fold in the chocolate and spoon the mixture into 12 x ½ cup (125ml/4 fl oz) capacity muffin tins lined with paper patty cases. Bake for 20–25 minutes or until cooked when tested with a skewer. Makes 12.

## lamingtons

2 x 20cm (8 in) square sponge cakes (recipe, page 89)
3 cups (450g/15¾ oz) icing (confectioner's) sugar, sifted
¾ cup (90g/3 oz) cocoa powder, sifted
1 cup (250ml/8 fl oz) boiling water
¼ cup (60ml/2 fl oz) milk
75g (2½ oz) melted butter
desiccated coconut, to coat

Cut the sponge into 6cm (2¼ in) squares. Mix together the icing sugar, cocoa, water, milk and butter in a large bowl. Place the coconut in another bowl. Roll the sponge squares in the icing and then in the desiccated coconut. Place on a baking tray lined with non-stick baking paper and refrigerate until set. Makes 18.

lamingtons

raspberry and white chocolate muffins          whipped white chocolate pastries

chocolate madeleines

## raspberry and white chocolate muffins

2 cups (300g/10½ oz) self-raising (self-rising) flour, sifted
¾ cup (165g/5¾ oz) caster (superfine) sugar
1 cup (250g/8 oz) sour cream
2 eggs
1 teaspoon finely grated lemon rind
⅓ cup (80ml/2½ fl oz) vegetable oil
1½ cups raspberries, fresh or frozen+
1 cup chopped white chocolate

Preheat the oven to 180°C (350°F). Place the flour and sugar into a bowl and mix to combine. Combine the sour cream, eggs, lemon rind and oil and whisk together. Stir the sour cream mixture into the flour mixture until just combined. Fold through the raspberries and chocolate and spoon the mixture into 8 x 1 cup (250ml/8 fl oz) capacity muffin tins lined with paper patty cases. Bake for 25–30 minutes or until cooked when tested with a skewer. Makes 8.
+ If using frozen raspberries, there is no need to defrost them first.

## whipped white chocolate pastries

375g (13¼ oz) store-bought puff pastry block
400g (14 oz) white chocolate, chopped
1 cup (250ml/8 fl oz) (single or pouring) cream
1 teaspoon vanilla extract

Preheat the oven to 200°C (390°F). Roll out the pastry on a lightly floured surface to a 3cm (1 in) thick, 12 x 40cm (4¾ x 15¾ in) rectangle. Cut the pastry into 8 strips 5cm (2 in) wide. Place on a baking tray lined with non-stick baking paper and bake for 20 minutes or until puffed and golden. Cool on a wire rack. Place the chocolate, cream and vanilla in a small saucepan over low heat. Stir until the chocolate is melted. Place the chocolate mixture in the bowl of electric mixer and beat for 15 minutes or until cooled and thick and fluffy. Split the pastries in half and fill with the whipped chocolate. Serves 8.

## chocolate madeleines

2 eggs
⅓ cup (75g/2½ oz) caster (superfine) sugar
⅓ cup (50g/1¾ oz) plain (all-purpose) flour
1 teaspoon baking powder
2 tablespoons cocoa powder
60g (2 oz) butter, melted

Preheat the oven to 180°C (350°F). Place the eggs and sugar in a bowl and whisk to combine. Sift the flour, baking powder and cocoa over the egg mixture and fold through with the melted butter. Spoon the mixture into greased large madeleine tins until two-thirds full. Bake for 10 minutes or until the madeleines are set. Makes 12.

## butterfly cakes with crushed-berry cream

125g (4 oz) butter, softened
¾ cup (165g/5¾ oz) caster (superfine) sugar
2 eggs
1¼ cups (190g/6¾ oz) self-raising (self-rising) flour
2 tablespoons cocoa powder
½ cup (125ml/4 fl oz) milk
100g (3½ oz) milk chocolate, melted
*crushed-berry cream*
125g (4 oz) fresh raspberries
1¼ cups (300ml/9½ fl oz) double cream
1 tablespoon icing (confectioner's) sugar, sifted

Preheat the oven to 160°C (320°F). Place the butter and sugar in the bowl of an electric mixer and beat until light and creamy. Gradually add eggs and beat well. Sift over flour and cocoa powder and beat until combined. Fold through the milk and chocolate and spoon the mixture into 12 x ½ cup (125ml/4 fl oz) capacity muffin tins lined with paper patty cases. Bake for 20–25 minutes or until cooked when tested with a skewer. Cool on wire racks.

To make the crushed-berry cream, place the raspberries in a bowl and lightly crush with a fork. Fold through the cream and icing sugar. Cut the tops out of the cupcakes and fill the holes with the berry cream. Top with the cupcake lids. Makes 12.

butterfly cakes with crushed-berry cream

## flourless chocolate cupcakes with chocolate glaze

200g (7 oz) dark cooking chocolate, chopped
160g (5½ oz) butter, chopped
5 eggs, separated
1½ cups (165g/5¾ oz) almond meal
¾ cup (165g/5¾ oz) sugar
1 quantity chocolate glaze (recipe, page 14)

Preheat the oven to 170°C (340°F). Place the chocolate and butter in a small saucepan over low heat and stir until the chocolate is melted and smooth. Allow to cool slightly, then stir in the egg yolks, almond meal and ½ cup of the sugar. Set aside. Place the egg whites in a separate bowl and beat with an electric beater until soft peaks form. Gradually add the remaining sugar and beat until glossy. Fold the egg white mixture into the chocolate mixture. Spoon the mixture into 6 x 1 cup (250ml/8 fl oz) capacity lightly greased muffin tins. Bake for 30 minutes or until cooked when tested with a skewer. Set aside to cool. Spoon the chocolate glaze over the cooled cupcakes. Makes 6.

## short-black cupcakes

125g (4 oz) butter, softened
¾ cup (165g/5¾ oz) caster (superfine) sugar
2 eggs
1¼ cups (190g/6¾ oz) self-raising (self-rising) flour
2 tablespoons cocoa powder
½ cup (125ml/4 fl oz) milk
100g (3½ oz) dark chocolate, melted
*coffee icing*
1 cup (220g/7¾ oz) caster (superfine) sugar
¼ cup (60ml/2 fl oz) water
¼ teaspoon cream of tartar
2 tablespoons instant coffee granules or powder
3 egg whites

Preheat the oven to 160°C (320°F). Place the butter and sugar in the bowl of an electric mixer and beat until light and creamy. Gradually add the eggs and beat well. Sift over the flour and cocoa, and beat until combined. Fold through the milk, stir in the chocolate and spoon the mixture into 4 x 12 hole 25ml (¾ fl oz) capacity mini-muffin tins lined with paper patty cases. Bake for 10–12 minutes or until cooked when tested with a skewer. Cool on wire racks.

To make the coffee icing, place the sugar, water, cream of tartar and coffee in a saucepan over high heat and stir until the sugar is dissolved. Bring to the boil, reduce the heat to low and simmer for 3 minutes. Place the egg whites in the bowl of an electric mixer and beat until soft peaks form. While the motor is still running, gradually add the sugar mixture and beat until thick and glossy. Spread the icing over the cupcakes with a palette knife. Makes 48.

flourless chocolate cupcakes with chocolate glaze

short-black cupcakes

espresso cakes

sweet chocolate buns

double chocolate éclairs

## espresso cakes

100g (3½ oz) butter, very well softened
1 cup (220g/7¾ oz) caster (superfine) sugar
3 eggs
1¼ cups (190g/6¾ oz) plain (all-purpose) flour, sifted
2 teaspoons baking powder
¼ cup (30g/1 oz) hazelnut meal (see glossary)
1½ tablespoons instant coffee granules or powder
dissolved in 1 tablespoon boiling water
1 quantity chocolate glaze (recipe, page 14)

Preheat the oven to 160°C (320°F). Place the butter, sugar, eggs, flour, baking powder, hazelnut meal and coffee mixture in a bowl. Combine using electric beaters on low speed, then increase to high speed and mix until just smooth. Grease 10 x ½ cup (125ml/4 fl oz) capacity muffin or patty tins. Spoon in the mixture and bake for 25 minutes or until cooked when tested with a skewer. Cool cakes in the tins for 10 minutes then remove and cool on a wire rack. Pour chocolate glaze over cooled cakes. Makes 10.

## sweet chocolate buns

1 quantity basic sweet dough (recipe, page 90)
80g (2¾ oz) dark chocolate, chopped
1 egg yolk
2 tablespoons (single or pouring) cream
caster (superfine) sugar for sprinkling

Preheat the oven to 160°C (320°F). Divide the dough into 6 pieces and roll into balls. Press out into oval shapes measuring 11 x 9cm (4¼ x 3½ in). Place the chocolate in the centre and fold to enclose. Place in 6 greased 9 x 4.5cm (3½ x 1¾ in) loaf tins, cover with a clean tea towel and set aside in a warm place for 1 hour or until doubled in size. Whisk together the egg yolk and cream and brush over the loaves. Sprinkle with the sugar and bake for 20 minutes or until golden. Serve warm. Makes 6.

## double chocolate éclairs

1 cup (250ml/8 fl oz) water
100g (3½ oz) butter, chopped
¾ cup (120g/4¼ oz) plain (all-purpose) flour
5 eggs
1 quantity chocolate crème pâtissière (recipe, page 88)
melted dark chocolate, for topping

Preheat the oven to 180°C (350°C). Place the water and butter in a saucepan over high heat and cook until butter is melted and the mixture starts to simmer. Add the flour and beat with a wooden spoon until smooth. Cook, stirring over low heat until the mixture leaves the side of the pan. Remove from heat and place in the bowl of an electric mixer. Add eggs gradually, beating on high speed until well combined. Spoon mixture into a piping bag with a 12mm (½ in) plain nozzle. Pipe 8cm (3 in) lengths of mixture onto baking trays lined with non-stick baking paper. Bake for 20–25 minutes or until golden. Cool on wire racks. Halve éclairs and fill bases with chocolate crème pâtissière. Dip the tops in chocolate, allow to set. Sandwich tops to bases. Makes 12.

## double chocolate cupcakes

125g (4 oz) butter, softened
¾ cup (165g/5¾ oz) caster (superfine) sugar
2 eggs
1¼ cups (190g/6¾ oz) plain (all-purpose) flour
1 teaspoon baking powder
2 tablespoons cocoa powder
½ cup (125ml/4 fl oz) milk
100g (3½ oz) dark chocolate, melted
1 quantity chocolate fudge icing (recipe, page 15)

Preheat the oven to 160°C (320°F). Place the butter and sugar in the bowl of an electric mixer and beat until light and creamy. Gradually add eggs and beat well. Sift over flour, baking powder and cocoa and beat until combined. Fold through the milk and chocolate and spoon the mixture into 12 x ½ cup (125ml/4 fl oz) capacity muffin tins lined with paper patty cases. Bake for 20–25 minutes or until cooked when tested with a skewer. Cool on wire racks. Spread or pipe the chocolate fudge icing over the cupcakes and refrigerate until serving. Makes 12.

double chocolate cupcakes

## chocolate and hazelnut coffee cakes

375g (13¼ oz) butter, softened
1½ cups (265g/9¼ oz) brown sugar
3 eggs
1 cup (150g/5¼ oz) plain (all-purpose) flour, sifted
2 teaspoons baking powder
⅔ cup (80g/3 oz) cocoa powder, sifted
1 cup (110g/3¾ oz) hazelnut meal (see glossary), sifted
¾ cup (185ml/6 fl oz) milk
⅓ cup instant coffee granules or powder
    dissolved in 1 tablespoon boiling water

Preheat the oven to 160°C (320°F). Place the butter and sugar in the bowl of an electric mixer and beat for 8–10 minutes or until light and creamy. Gradually add the eggs and beat well. Fold through the flour, baking powder, cocoa and hazelnut meal and stir in the milk and coffee mixture. Spoon the mixture into 8 x ¾ cup (185ml/6 fl oz) capacity well-greased ovenproof dishes and bake for 40 minutes or until cooked when tested with a skewer. Serve with vanilla ice-cream and hazelnut liqueur, if desired. Makes 8.

## raspberry macaroon tarts

3 egg whites
¾ cup (165g/5¾ oz) sugar
3 cups (225g/7⅞ oz) desiccated coconut
*raspberry chocolate filling*
½ cup (125ml/4 fl oz) (single or pouring) cream
125g (4 oz) dark chocolate, chopped
2 eggs
2 tablespoons caster (superfine) sugar
2 tablespoons self-raising (self-rising) flour, sifted
200g (7 oz) raspberries, fresh or frozen+

Preheat the oven to 140°C (280°F). Combine the egg whites, sugar and coconut to make the macaroon mixture and divide between 6 x 8cm (3¼ in) well-greased tart tins with removable bases. Press firmly over the base and sides. Bake for 25–30 minutes or until the macaroon shells are firm.

To make the filling, place the cream and chocolate in a saucepan over low heat and stir until smooth. Set aside. Place the eggs and sugar in the bowl of an electric mixer and beat until light and creamy. Fold through the flour and the chocolate mixture. Spoon the mixture into the macaroon shells and top with the raspberries. Bake at 160°C (320°F) for 25 minutes or until the filling is just firm. Cool in the tins. Makes 6.

+ If using frozen raspberries, there is no need to defrost before using.

chocolate and hazelnut coffee cakes

raspberry macaroon tarts

# cakes

Turn whatever occasion you have to celebrate, be it
a birthday, anniversary, morning or afternoon tea, into
a special event by serving a big, luscious chocolate cake.
So rise to the occasion and become the homecook hero
who can always be counted on to make a sensational
cake. Your reward will be the chorus of oohs and aahs
that greets the presentation of your masterpiece. Not
to mention the deep satisfaction of sampling a slice.

basic chocolate cake

melt-and-mix chocolate coconut cake

chocolate sponge cake

## basic chocolate cake

375g (13¼ oz) butter, softened
1½ cups (260g/9 oz) brown sugar
3 eggs
2 cups (300g/10½ oz) plain (all-purpose) flour, sifted
2 teaspoons baking powder
⅔ cup (80g/3 oz) cocoa, double sifted
¾ cup (185ml/6 fl oz) milk
1 quantity chocolate glaze (recipe, page 14)

Preheat the oven to 160°C (320°F). Place the butter and sugar in the bowl of an electric mixer and beat for 8–10 minutes or until light and creamy. Gradually add the eggs and beat well. Fold through the flour, baking powder and cocoa and stir in the milk. Spoon the mixture into a 22cm (8½ in) round cake tin lined with non-stick baking paper and bake for 1 hour and 10 minutes or until cooked when tested with a skewer. Cool in the tin for 10 minutes then turn out onto a wire rack. Ice with chocolate glaze. Serves 8–10.

## melt-and-mix chocolate coconut cake

250g (8 oz) butter, melted
¾ cup (90g/3 oz) cocoa powder, sifted
1⅓ cups (295g/10½ oz) caster (superfine) sugar
4 eggs
1½ cups desiccated coconut
1½ cups (225g/7⅞ oz) self-raising (self-rising) flour, sifted
1 teaspoon baking powder
¾ cup (185ml/6 fl oz) milk
1 quantity chocolate glaze (recipe, page 14)

Preheat the oven to 160°C (320°F). Combine all the ingredients in a bowl and whisk until smooth. Pour into a 20cm (8 in) square cake tin which has been lined with non-stick baking paper. Bake for 1 hour, or until cooked when tested with a skewer. Allow to cool in the tin for 10 minutes then turn onto a wire rack. When completely cool, spread with chocolate glaze. Serves 8–10.

## chocolate sponge cake

⅓ cup (40g/1½ oz) plain (all-purpose) flour
⅓ cup (40g/1½ oz) cocoa powder
¼ teaspoon baking powder
4 eggs
½ cup (110g/3¾ oz) caster (superfine) sugar
50g (1¾ oz) butter, melted

Preheat the oven to 180°C (350°F). Sift the flour, cocoa and baking powder three times. Set aside. Place the eggs and sugar in the bowl of an electric mixer and beat for 8–10 minutes or until the mixture has tripled in volume. Sift half the flour mixture over the egg mixture and gently fold in using a metal spoon. Repeat with the remaining flour. Add the butter and fold through. Grease two shallow 19cm (7½ in) round cake tins and line the bases with non-stick baking paper. Divide the mixture between the tins and bake for 25 minutes or until cakes are springy to touch and come away from the sides of the tin. Remove from the tins and place on wire racks to cool. To serve, fill cake with any combination of jam (jelly), whipped cream or berries. Serves 8.

## melt-and-mix white chocolate mud cake

250g (8 oz) butter, chopped
200g (7 oz) white chocolate, chopped
2¼ cups (495g/15⅞ oz) caster (superfine) sugar
1½ cups (375ml/12 fl oz) water
2 cups (300g/10½ oz) plain (all-purpose) flour
⅔ cup (100g/3½ oz) self-raising (self-rising) flour
3 eggs, lightly beaten
1 teaspoon vanilla extract
1 quantity white chocolate fudge icing (recipe, page 15)

Preheat the oven to 120°C (250°F). Place the butter, chocolate, sugar and water in a saucepan over medium heat and stir until the mixture is smooth. Transfer mixture to a large bowl and whisk in the flours, then whisk in the eggs and vanilla. Pour the mixture into a 22cm (8½ in) round cake tin which has been lined with non-stick baking paper. Bake for 2 hours or until cooked when tested with a skewer. Stand in tin for 10 minutes before turning onto a wire rack to cool, then spread with white chocolate fudge icing. Serves 8–10.

melt-and-mix white chocolate mud cake

rich chocolate cake                    baked chocolate fudge cake

marble cake

## rich chocolate cake

300g (10½ oz) dark couverture (see basics), chopped
250g (8 oz) butter
5 eggs, separated
⅓ cup (75g/2¾ oz) caster (superfine) sugar
1 teaspoon vanilla extract
⅓ cup (50g/1¾ oz) plain (all-purpose) flour
½ teaspoon baking powder
1 quantity chocolate glaze (recipe, page 14)

Preheat the oven to 130°C (265°F). Place the chocolate and butter in a saucepan over low heat and stir until melted and smooth. Set aside. Place the egg yolks, sugar and vanilla in the bowl of an electric mixer and beat until thick and pale. Place the egg whites in a separate bowl and beat until stiff peaks form. Fold the chocolate mixture through the egg yolk mixture. Sift over the flour and baking powder and gently fold through. Carefully fold the egg whites through. Pour the mixture into a 20cm (8 in) round cake tin lined with non-stick baking paper. Bake for 1¼ hours or until firm. Cool in the tin. Spread the cooled cake with the glaze. Serve cake at room temperature, not chilled. Serves 8–10.

## baked chocolate fudge cake

400g (14 oz) dark couverture (see basics), chopped
120g (3⅞ oz) unsalted butter
1 cup (175g/6 oz) brown sugar
½ cup (125ml/4 fl oz) (single or pouring) cream
2 tablespoons instant coffee granules or powder
5 eggs
2 tablespoons plain (all-purpose) flour, sifted

Preheat the oven to 150°C (300°F). Place the chocolate, butter, sugar, cream and coffee in a medium saucepan over low heat and stir until the mixture is melted. Place the eggs and the flour in a bowl and whisk to combine. Slowly whisk the chocolate mixture into the egg mixture and pour into a lightly greased 7½ x 32½cm (3 x 13 in) rectangular tin lined with non-stick baking paper. Place the tin in a deep baking tray and pour in enough boiling water to come halfway up the sides of the tin. Bake for 2¼ hours or until it is cooked when tested with a skewer. Refrigerate until cooled completely. Serves 10.

## marble cake

250g (8 oz) butter, chopped
1¼ cups (275g/9½ oz) caster (superfine) sugar
1 teaspoon vanilla extract
3 eggs
2¼ cups (340g/12 oz) self-raising (self-rising) flour, sifted
¾ cup (180ml/6 fl oz) milk
4½ tablespoons cocoa powder, sifted
3 tablespoons caster (superfine) sugar, extra
1½ tablespoons milk, extra
1 quantity basic chocolate icing (recipe, page 14)

Preheat the oven to 180°C (350°F). Place the butter, sugar and vanilla in the bowl of an electric mixer and beat until light and creamy. Add the eggs and beat well. Fold through the flour and milk. Divide the mixture in 2. Stir the cocoa and extra sugar and milk through one portion. Grease a 22cm (8½ in) round bundt tin. Drop alternate spoonfuls of plain and chocolate cake mixture, then swirl with a knife. Bake for 45 minutes or until the cake is cooked when tested with a skewer. Cool on a wire rack. Ice the cooled cake. Serves 8–10.

## chocolate mud cake

375g (13½ oz) butter, softened
1⅓ cups (230g/7⅞ oz) brown sugar
3 eggs
2 cups (300g/10½ oz) plain (all-purpose) flour, sifted
½ teaspoon baking powder
⅔ cup (80g/3 oz) cocoa powder, double sifted
200g (7 oz) dark chocolate, melted
¾ cup (180ml/6 fl oz) milk

Preheat the oven to 160°C (320°F). Place the butter and sugar in the bowl of an electric mixer and beat for 8–10 minutes, or until the mixture is light and creamy. Gradually add the eggs and beat well. Fold through the flour, baking powder, cocoa and melted chocolate and stir in the milk. Spoon the mixture into a 22cm (8½ in) round cake tin lined with non-stick baking paper and bake for 1¼ hours or until cooked when tested with a skewer. Cool in the tin. To serve, dust with cocoa and serve with cream. Serves 10.

chocolate mud cake

# layered chocolate cake

220g (7¾ oz) unsalted butter, softened

2 cups (440g/15½ oz) caster (superfine) sugar

1 teaspoon vanilla extract

4 eggs

2 cups (300g/10½ oz) plain (all-purpose) flour, sifted

½ cup (60g/2 oz) cocoa powder, sifted

2½ teaspoons baking powder

½ teaspoon salt

1 cup (250ml/8 fl oz) milk

2 tablespoons instant coffee granules or powder
   dissolved in 1½ tablespoons boiling water

750g (1½ lb) mascarpone cheese

¾ cup (120g/3⅞ oz) icing (confectioner's) sugar, sifted

⅓ cup (80ml/2½ fl oz) coffee-flavoured liqueur

1 quantity chocolate truffle icing (recipe, page 89)

Preheat the oven to 160°C (320°F). Place the butter, sugar and vanilla in the bowl of an electric mixer and beat for 10–12 minutes or until light and creamy. Gradually add the eggs and beat well. Fold through the flour, cocoa, baking powder, salt and milk. Spoon the mixture into 2 lightly greased 20cm (8 in) round cake tins lined with non-stick baking paper and cook for 45–50 minutes or until cooked when tested with a skewer. Stand in the tin for 10 minutes then turn out onto a wire rack to cool. Place the mascarpone, sugar and coffee mixture in a bowl and stir well to combine. Set aside. To assemble the cake, cut each cake in half horizontally to make four layers and brush off any crumbs using a pastry brush. Place one cake layer on a plate, spoon over 2 tablespoons of liqueur and spread over 1 cup of mascarpone mixture. Top with another cake layer and repeat with the remaining ingredients. Use a palette knife to spread the chocolate truffle icing over the top and sides of the cake. Serves 12.

# chocolate cheesecake

250g (8oz) store-bought chocolate biscuits

100g (3½ oz) butter, melted

450g (15½ oz) dark chocolate, chopped

50g (1¾ oz) butter, extra

2 tablespoons cocoa powder

675g (1½ lb) cream cheese, softened

1 cup (220g/7¾ oz) caster (superfine) sugar

4 eggs

1½ cups (375g/13¼ oz) sour cream

2 teaspoons vanilla extract

fresh raspberries, to serve

Preheat the oven to 180°C (350°F). Place the chocolate biscuits in a food processor and process until fine. Add the melted butter and process until well blended. Press the mixture into the bottom of a 22cm (8½ in) round springform cake tin which has been lined with non-stick baking paper. Bake for 8 minutes, remove from oven and allow to cool. Place the chocolate and extra butter in a saucepan over low heat and stir until melted. Whisk in the cocoa and set aside. Place the cream cheese and sugar in the bowl of an electric mixer and beat until fluffy. Add eggs gradually. Add chocolate mixture and beat well. Add sour cream and vanilla and beat well. Pour into tin and wrap the outside of the tin with foil. Place tin in a roasting dish and fill with hot water, so that it comes halfway up the side of the cake tin. Bake for 45 minutes. Remove from oven and leave to cool in the water bath for 15 minutes. Loosely cover and refrigerate for 12 hours. To serve, cut into slices and top with raspberries. Serves 12.

layered chocolate cake

chocolate cheesecake

simple choc hazelnut layer cake                    chocolate cake with orange syrup

devil's food cake

## simple choc hazelnut layer cake

2 x 20cm (8 in) quality store-bought sponge cakes
1 cup chocolate hazelnut spread
*topping*
1¼ cups (310ml/10 fl oz) double (heavy) cream
¼ cup (40g/1½ oz) icing (confectioner's) sugar
1 cup chocolate hazelnut spread

Cut each sponge cake into 2 layers. Spread each layer thinly with
the chocolate hazelnut spread and sandwich together.

To make the topping, place the cream, icing sugar and chocolate
hazelnut spread in a bowl. Fold gently to combine and spread over
the top and sides of the cake. Serves 8–10.

## chocolate cake with orange syrup

8 eggs
1⅓ cups (295g/10½ oz) caster (superfine) sugar
⅔ cup (80g/2⅞ oz) cocoa powder, sifted
1 cup (150g/5¼ oz) plain (all-purpose) flour, sifted
75g butter, melted
*orange syrup*
½ cup orange zest
1 cup (250ml/8 fl oz) water
1 cup (250ml/8 fl oz) orange juice
1½ cups (330g/11½ oz) sugar

Preheat the oven to 160°C (320°F). Line a deep 20cm (8 in) round
cake tin lined with non-stick baking paper. Place the eggs and sugar
in the bowl of an electric mixer and beat for 7–8 minutes until the
mixture is light and fluffy. Add the cocoa, flour and butter, folding
gently until just combined. Pour mixture into the cake tin, bake for
1¼ hours or until cooked when tested with a skewer.

While the cake is cooking, make the orange syrup. Heat the zest,
water, juice and sugar in a saucepan over medium heat, stirring until
the sugar has dissolved. Allow the syrup to simmer for 8 minutes or
until thick. Cool the cake in the tin for 5 minutes, turn out and place
on a serving plate. Pour the syrup and zest over the top of the cake
and serve warm. Serves 8.

## devil's food cake

185g (6½ oz) butter, softened
1¾ cups (385g/13½ oz) caster (superfine) sugar
1½ teaspoons vanilla extract
3 eggs
½ cup (125ml/4 fl oz) buttermilk
⅓ cup (80ml/2½ fl oz) water
½ teaspoon red food colouring
2 cups (300g/10½ oz) plain (all-purpose) flour, sifted
⅔ cup (80g/2⅞ oz) cocoa powder, sifted
1¼ teaspoons bicarbonate of soda (baking soda), sifted
1 quantity chocolate ganache (recipe, page 15)

Preheat the oven to 160°C (320°F). Place the butter, sugar and vanilla
in the bowl of an electric mixer and beat until light and fluffy. Add
eggs gradually and beat well. Combine the buttermilk, water and food
colouring in a bowl. Fold the flour, cocoa and bicarbonate of soda
through the butter mixture, then fold the buttermilk mixture through.
Divide mixture between 2 x 20cm (8 in) round cake tins which have
been lined with non-stick baking paper. Bake for 50 minutes or until
cooked when tested with a skewer. Cool cakes on wire racks. Spread
the tops of cakes with ganache and sandwich together. Serves 10.

## choc-chip butter cake

185g (6½ oz) butter, softened
1¼ cups (275g/9½ oz) caster (superfine) sugar
1 teaspoon vanilla extract
4 eggs
¾ cup (190g/6¾ oz) sour cream
2⅓ cups (350g/12¼ oz) plain (all-purpose) flour
1¼ teaspoons baking powder
¾ cup chopped dark chocolate

Preheat the oven to 160°C (320°F). Place butter, sugar and vanilla in
the bowl of an electric mixer and beat for 8–10 minutes, or until light
and creamy. Add the eggs and sour cream and beat well. Fold through
the flour, baking powder and chocolate. Spoon the mixture into a
20 x 30cm (8 x 12 in) slab tin lined with non-stick baking paper. Bake
for 40 minutes or until cooked when tested with a skewer. Serves 9.

choc-chip butter cake

## milk chocolate and coffee layer cake

1 quantity basic meringue mixture (recipe, page 89)
½ cup almond meal (ground almonds)
400g (14 oz) milk chocolate
½ cup (125ml/4 fl oz) (single or pouring) cream
2 teaspoons instant coffee granules or powder
1½ cups (375ml/12 fl oz) (single or pouring) cream, whipped

Preheat the oven to 120°C (250°F). Place the basic meringue mixture in a bowl and fold through the almond meal until well combined. Draw 3 x 20cm (8 in) circles on 3 pieces of non-stick baking paper and place on individual baking trays. Divide the mixture between the circles and spread it out evenly with a butter knife. Cook for 25 minutes or until the meringue is crisp to touch. Turn off the oven and allow to cool in the oven for 30 minutes. Place the chocolate, cream and coffee in a small saucepan over low heat and stir until the chocolate is melted and smooth. Allow to cool. To assemble, spread one meringue round with the chocolate mixture and top with a layer of the whipped cream. Repeat with the remaining meringues, chocolate and cream and finish with a layer of cream. Serves 6.

## chocolate mousse cake

⅓ cup (50g/1¾ oz) plain (all-purpose) flour
⅛ teaspoon baking powder
2 eggs
¼ cup (55g/1⅞ oz) caster (superfine) sugar
25g (⅞ oz) butter, melted
1 tablespoon sherry
1 quantity chocolate mousse filling (recipe, page 88)
cocoa powder, sifted, for dusting
white chocolate shavings, to serve

Preheat the oven to 180°C (350°F). Sift the flour and baking powder three times. Set aside. Place the eggs and sugar in the bowl of an electric mixer and beat for 8–10 minutes or until mixture is thick, pale and tripled in volume. Sift the flour mixture over the egg mixture and gently fold through. Add the butter and fold through. Grease a 22cm (8½ in) round cake tin and line the base with non-stick baking paper. Pour the mixture into the tin and bake for 20 minutes or until cake comes away from the sides. Remove from tin and cool on a wire rack. Trim the sponge to fit the base of a 20cm (8 in) round springform tin which has been lined with non-stick baking paper. Press the sponge in, sprinkle with the sherry and top with chocolate mousse filling. Refrigerate for 2 hours or until set. To serve, dust with cocoa and top with white chocolate shavings. Serves 8–10.

milk chocolate and coffee layer cake

chocolate mousse cake

# desserts

Music may be the food of love, but there are few greater
treats you can give family and friends than a sensational
homemade dessert. Add chocolate to the score and
you'll have entered the realm of paying them ultimate
compliments. Play on through this repertoire of tarts,
puddings and ices and you'll have your guests lining up
for seconds. You don't need to let on how simple they
really are to prepare.

molten chocolate puddings

crushed-praline truffle                    chocolate brioche French toast

## molten chocolate puddings

150g (5¼ oz) dark chocolate
100g (3½ oz) unsalted butter
2 eggs
2 egg yolks
¼ cup (55g/1⅞ oz) caster (superfine) sugar
2 tablespoons plain (all-purpose) flour, sifted
thick (double) cream to serve

Preheat the oven to 180°C (350°F). Place the chocolate and butter in a saucepan over low heat and stir until the chocolate is melted and smooth. Place the eggs, yolks and sugar in a bowl and whisk until pale. Gently fold in the flour and chocolate mixture and spoon into 4 lightly greased 1 cup (250ml/8 fl oz) capacity ovenproof dishes. Bake for 12–15 minutes or until the puddings are puffed. Top with the cream to serve. Serves 4.

## crushed-praline truffle

¾ cup (165g/5¾ oz) caster (superfine) sugar
⅓ cup (80ml/2½ fl oz) water
⅓ cup macadamia nuts, roasted until golden
⅓ cup (80ml/2½ fl oz) (single or pouring) cream
350g (12¼ oz) dark chocolate, chopped

To make the praline, line 2 baking trays with non-stick baking paper. Place the sugar and water in a small saucepan over low heat and stir without boiling. Brush any sugar crystals from the inside of the pan with a pastry brush dipped in water. When the sugar is dissolved, increase the heat and bring to the boil. Boil for 8–10 minutes or until dark golden. Remove from the heat, allow the bubbles to subside, and pour one-third of the toffee over the nuts and the remainder onto the other baking tray. Leave to set. To crush the praline, place the set toffee with macadamias into a food processor and process until finely chopped. Set aside. Place the cream in a saucepan over low heat and bring almost to the boil. Add the chocolate and stir for 1 minute or until smooth. Stir through the crushed praline. Pour into a greased 15 x 9 x 10cm (6 x 3½ x 4 in) loaf tin lined with non-stick baking paper. Refrigerate for 2 hours or until set. Turn out onto a plate, coarsely chop the plain toffee and sprinkle over the top. Serves 10.

## chocolate brioche French toast

8 slices brioche
125g (4 oz) dark chocolate, melted
2 eggs
½ cup (125ml/4 fl oz) milk
¼ cup (55g/1⅞ oz) caster (superfine) sugar
1 teaspoon vanilla extract
butter for greasing the pan

Spread 4 slices of the brioche with the melted chocolate and sandwich together with the remaining brioche slices. Whisk together the eggs, milk, sugar and vanilla in a bowl. Heat a greased frying pan over medium heat. Very quickly, dip a brioche sandwich into the egg mixture and place in the pan. Cook for 2–3 minutes each side or until crispy golden brown. Repeat with the remaining sandwiches. Serves 4.

## bitter chocolate meringue tart

200g (7 oz) store-bought shortbread biscuits
1 tablespoon cocoa powder
50g (1¾ oz) butter, melted
*bitter chocolate filling*
400g (14 oz) 70% cocoa dark chocolate, melted
1 cup (250ml/8 fl oz) (single or pouring) cream
*meringue top*
150ml (4¾ fl oz) egg whites (approximately 4)
1 cup (220g/7¾ oz) caster (superfine) sugar

Place the biscuits, cocoa and butter in a food processor and process for 2–3 minutes or until the mixture resembles fine breadcrumbs. Press the mixture into a 20cm (8 in) loose-bottomed round fluted tart tin to create the tart base. Refrigerate for 15 minutes.

To make the chocolate filling, place the chocolate and cream in a small saucepan over low heat and stir until melted and smooth. Pour over the biscuit base and refrigerate for 30 minutes or until set.

To make the meringue top, preheat the oven to 200°C (400°F). Place the egg whites in the bowl of an electric mixer and beat until soft peaks form. Gradually add the sugar and beat until the mixture is thick and glossy. Spoon meringue onto the tart and bake for 15 minutes or until the peaks are golden and the meringue is set. Cool. Serves 8.

bitter chocolate meringue tart

chocolate sorbet

chocolate tiramisu

chocolate soufflé

## chocolate sorbet

5 cups (1¼L/2 pints) water
1½ cups (260g/9 oz) brown sugar
1 cup (220g/7¾ oz) caster (superfine) sugar
1⅓ cups (160g/5½ oz) cocoa powder
¼ teaspoon salt
220g (7¾ oz) dark chocolate, finely chopped
2 teaspoons vanilla extract

Place the water, brown sugar, sugar, cocoa and salt in a saucepan and bring to the boil, stirring to dissolve sugars. Remove from heat, stir through chocolate until smooth. Pour through a fine strainer into a bowl, stir through vanilla and set aside to cool slightly. Transfer mixture into an ice-cream maker and freeze according to manufacturer's instructions. Serves 4.

## chocolate tiramisu

½ cup (125ml/4 fl oz) (single or pouring) cream
300g (10½ oz) dark chocolate, chopped
1½ cups (375ml/12 fl oz) (single or pouring) cream, extra
1½ cups (375g/12 oz) mascarpone cheese
2 tablespoons coffee-flavoured liqueur
⅓ cup (80ml/2½ fl oz) espresso coffee, cooled
12 store-bought sponge finger biscuits

Line a 32 x 7 x 8cm (12¾ x 2¾ x 3¼ in) bar tin with non-stick baking paper. Place the cream and chocolate in a small saucepan over low heat and stir until the chocolate is melted. Set aside to cool. Whisk together the extra cream and mascarpone until light and fluffy. In a separate bowl, combine the liqueur and coffee and quickly dip both sides of the biscuits in the mixture. Pour one-third of the chocolate mixture into the tin and top with one-third of the cream and half the biscuits. Top with another third of the cream followed by the remaining biscuits and cream. Pour over another third of the chocolate mixture and set the remaining third aside. Cover the tiramisu with plastic wrap and place in the fridge for 3 hours or until set. To serve, warm the remaining chocolate mixture in a small saucepan over low heat. Carefully invert the tiramisu and serve the warm chocolate separately. Serves 6.

## chocolate soufflé

melted butter, for brushing
caster (superfine) sugar, for dusting
150g (5¼ oz) dark chocolate, chopped
⅓ cup (80ml/2½ fl oz) (single or pouring) cream
¼ cup (30g/1 oz) cocoa powder, sifted
6 egg whites
½ cup (110g/3¾ oz) caster (superfine) sugar, extra

Preheat the oven to 180°C (350°F). Brush 4 x 1 cup (250ml/8 fl oz) capacity dishes with butter and dust with caster sugar. Place on a baking tray. Melt chocolate, cream and cocoa in a saucepan over low heat, stirring until smooth. Place egg whites in the bowl of an electric mixer and whisk until soft peaks form. Gradually add extra sugar and whisk until thick and glossy. Fold a quarter of the egg white mixture through the chocolate mixture. Gently fold remaining egg whites through and spoon into prepared dishes. Bake for 20 minutes or until soufflés are puffed and set. Serve the soufflés immediately. Serves 4.

## chocolate truffles

400g (14 oz) dark chocolate, finely chopped
¾ cup (180ml/6 fl oz) (single or pouring) cream
cocoa powder, sifted for dusting

Place the chocolate and cream in a small saucepan over low heat. Stir until the chocolate is melted and smooth. Pour the chocolate mixture into a 15 x 18cm (6 x 7 in) dish lined with non-stick baking paper. Place in the refrigerator for 2–3 hours or until set. Roll tablespoons of the mixture into balls and dust with the cocoa to serve. Makes 35.

chocolate truffles

## chocolate panna cotta

2 tablespoons water
2 teaspoons gelatine powder
2 cups (500ml/16 fl oz) (single or pouring) cream
⅓ cup (50g/1¾ oz) icing (confectioner's) sugar, sifted
100g (3½ oz) dark chocolate, chopped
vegetable oil, for greasing
mixed berries, to serve

Place the water in a bowl and sprinkle over the gelatine. Stand for 5 minutes or until the gelatine absorbs the water. Place the cream in a saucepan over medium heat with the sugar and chocolate. Stir to melt the chocolate, allowing the cream to come to the boil. Add the gelatine and cook, stirring, for 1–2 minutes to dissolve the gelatine. Strain the mixture and pour into 4 x ½ cup (4 fl oz) capacity moulds that have been very lightly greased with vegetable oil. Refrigerate for 4–6 hours or until firm. Remove the panna cotta from the fridge 5 minutes before serving, then unmould and serve with mixed berries. Serves 4.

## triple chocolate semifreddo

250g (8 oz) dark couverture chocolate, chopped
3 eggs
2 egg yolks
½ cup (110g/3¾ oz) caster (superfine) sugar
1¾ cups (430ml/13¾ fl oz) (single or pouring) cream
½ cup chopped white chocolate
½ cup chopped milk chocolate

Place the dark chocolate in a heatproof bowl over a saucepan of simmering water and stir until melted and smooth. Set aside. Place the eggs, yolks and sugar in a heatproof bowl over a saucepan of simmering water and whisk for 4–5 minutes or until the mixture is thick and pale. Remove from the heat and beat with an electric mixer for 5–6 minutes or until cool. Fold through the melted dark chocolate and set aside. Place the cream in the bowl of an electric mixer and beat until soft peaks form. Fold the egg and chocolate mixture and the white and milk chocolate through the cream. Pour the mixture into a metal bowl or cake tin, cover and freeze for 4–6 hours or until firm. To serve, place scoops of the semifreddo into chilled dishes. Serves 6–8.

chocolate panna cotta

triple chocolate semifreddo

## chocolate malt self-saucing pudding

130g (4½ oz) butter, softened
1¼ cups (275g/9½ oz) caster (superfine) sugar
2 eggs
1½ cups (225g/7⅞ oz) plain (all-purpose) flour
2¼ teaspoons baking powder
½ cup (60g/2 oz) cocoa powder
½ cup hazelnut meal (ground hazelnuts)
¼ cup malted milk powder
1 cup (250ml/8 fl oz) milk
*chocolate malt sauce*
⅔ cup (125g/4 oz) brown sugar
⅔ cup malted milk powder
1½ tablespoons cocoa powder
1½ cups (375ml/12 fl oz) boiling water

Preheat the oven to 170°C (340°F). Place the butter and sugar in the bowl of an electric mixer and beat until pale. Add the eggs gradually and beat until smooth. Sift the flour, baking powder and cocoa over the mixture, add the hazelnut meal, malted milk powder and milk and beat until smooth. Spoon the pudding mixture into a well greased 8 cup (2 litre/64 fl oz) capacity ovenproof baking dish.

To make the sauce, place the sugar, malted milk powder and cocoa in a bowl, pour over the boiling water and stir to combine. Spoon over the pudding mixture and bake for 45–50 minutes or until risen and cooked when tested with a skewer. Serves 6.

## white chocolate crème brûlée

1 cup (250ml/8 fl oz) (single or pouring) cream
¾ cup (180ml/6 fl oz) milk
4 egg yolks
¼ cup (55g/1⅞ oz) caster (superfine) sugar
90g (3 oz) white chocolate, melted
2 tablespoons caster (superfine) sugar, extra

Preheat the oven to 160°C (320°F). Place the cream and milk in a small saucepan over low heat and heat gently until the mixture just comes to the boil. Remove from the heat. Whisk the egg yolks and sugar together until thick and pale. Pour the warm cream mixture over the eggs and whisk to combine. Return to the pan and stir over low heat for 6–8 minutes or until the custard is thick enough to coat the back of a spoon. Remove from the heat and stir the custard into the melted chocolate. Pour the mixture into 4 x ½ cup (125ml/4 fl oz) capacity ovenproof ramekins and place in a deep baking dish. Pour in enough water to come halfway up the sides of the ramekins. Bake for 40 minutes or until just set. Remove and refrigerate for 3 hours or until set. Sprinkle each brûlée with one tablespoon of extra sugar. Heat a metal spoon over an open flame until very hot. Wearing an oven glove, remove the spoon from the heat and run it over the sugar on top of the brûlée to melt and caramelise it. Alternatively, use a kitchen blow torch to caramelise the sugar. Serves 4.

chocolate malt self-saucing pudding                   white chocolate crème brûlée

*glossary, index*

*+ conversions*

## almond meal

Also known as ground almonds, almond meal is available from most supermarkets. Used instead of, or as well as, flour in cakes and desserts. Make your own by processing whole skinned almonds to a fine meal in a food processor or blender (125g/4 oz almonds will give 1 cup almond meal). To remove the skins from almonds, briefly soak in boiling water, then using fingers, slip skins off.

## brioche

A sweet French yeast bread made in loaf or bun form. Traditionally dunked in coffee at breakfast. Available from speciality bread and cake stores and some supermarkets.

## butter

Unless stated otherwise in a recipe, butter should be at room temperature for cooking. It should not be half-melted or too soft to handle, but should still have some "give" when pressed. When using butter to make pastry, it should be cold and chopped into small pieces so that it can be evenly distributed throughout the flour. Although most bakers use unsalted rather than salted butter, it is a matter of personal preference and does not make much difference to the outcome. Salted butter has a much longer shelf-life, which makes it preferable for some people. Store butter in the fridge away from other foods with odours, mild or strong, as it is very easily tainted.

## basic butter cake

185g (6½ oz) butter, softened
1¼ cups (275g/9½ oz) caster
    (superfine) sugar
1 teaspoon vanilla extract
4 eggs
¾ cup (190g/6¾ oz) sour cream
2¼ cups (340g/12 oz) plain
    (all-purpose) flour, sifted
1¼ teaspoons baking powder

Preheat the oven to 160°C (320°F). Place the butter, sugar and vanilla in the bowl of an electric mixer and beat for 8–10 minutes or until light and creamy. Gradually add the eggs and sour cream and beat well. Fold through the flour and baking powder. Spoon the mixture into a 22cm (8½ in) round cake tin lined with non-stick baking paper. Cook for 1 hour 10 minutes or until cooked when tested with a skewer. Cool in the tin for 10 minutes, turn onto a wire rack. Serves 8.

## chocolate crème pâtissière

2 cups (500ml/16 fl oz) milk
200g (7 oz) chopped dark chocolate
1 teaspoon vanilla extract
4 egg yolks
⅓ cup (75g/2¾ oz) caster
    (superfine) sugar
⅓ cup (50g/1¾ oz) cornflour
    (cornstarch)

Place milk, chocolate and vanilla in a saucepan over medium–high heat and bring to the boil. Whisk together egg yolks and sugar until thick and pale. Add the cornflour and whisk to combine. Slowly pour in the hot milk, whisking continuously. Pour the mixture back into the saucepan over medium–high heat and simmer rapidly while whisking continuously for 5 minutes or until thick. Place a piece of non-stick baking paper directly onto the top of the pastry cream and set aside to cool. Makes 2⅓ cups.

## chocolate mousse filling

2 teaspoons powdered gelatine
2 tablespoons water
200g (7 oz) dark chocolate, chopped
75g (2¾ oz) butter, chopped
2 tablespoons cocoa powder, sifted
4 eggs, separated
1 cup (250ml/8 oz) (single
    or pouring) cream
3 tablespoons icing (confectioner's)
    sugar, sifted

Place the gelatine and water in a small bowl and set aside for 5 minutes to absorb. Place the chocolate, butter and cocoa in a saucepan over low heat and stir until melted and smooth. Remove from heat and stir the gelatine mixture through the chocolate mixture, until dissolved. Pour the mixture into a bowl and add the egg yolks gradually, beating well until combined. Set aside. Place the cream in the bowl of an electric mixer and whisk until soft peaks form. Set aside. Place the egg whites in the bowl of an electric mixer and whisk until soft peaks form. Gradually add icing sugar and whisk until thick and glossy. Gently fold the egg white mixture through the chocolate mixture and then fold the whipped cream through.

## chocolate topping

185g (6½ oz) dark chocolate
3 teaspoons vegetable oil

Place the chocolate and oil in a saucepan over low heat and stir until melted. Remove from the heat and allow to cool slightly before spreading over the slice. If you want to create a decorative pattern on the surface, run a comb or fork across the topping before it sets. It sets hard, so for a clean edge cut the slice with a warm knife which has been dipped in hot water.

## chocolate truffle icing

**400g (14 oz) dark chocolate, chopped**
**½ cup (125ml/4 fl oz) (single or**
**    pouring) cream**
Place the chocolate and cream in a small
saucepan over low heat and stir until
melted and smooth. Cool for 10 minutes.
Use a palette knife to spread the icing
over the cooled cake.

## cream

The fat content determines the names of
the different types of cream and the uses
for which they are ideal.

### single or pouring cream

Has a butter fat content of 20–30 per cent.
It is the type of cream most commonly
used for making ice-cream, panna cotta
and custard. It can also be whipped to a
light and airy consistency and served on
the side.

### thickened cream

Not to be mistaken for heavy or double
cream (below), this is single or pouring
cream that has had a vegetable gum
added to stabilise it. The gum makes the
cream a little thicker and easier to whip.

### heavy or double cream

Has a butter fat content of 40–50 per cent.
It is usually served on the side or on top of
cakes and desserts.

## eggs

The standard egg size used in this book
is 59g (2 oz). It is very important to
use the right size eggs for a recipe, as
this will affect the outcome of baked
goods. The correct volume is especially
important when using egg whites to make

meringues. Use eggs at room temperature
for baking so always remember to remove
them from the fridge about 30 minutes
before you begin.

## hazelnut meal

Also known as ground hazelnuts, meal
is available from many supermarkets
or make your own by processing whole
skinned hazelnuts to a fine meal in a
food processor or blender (125g/4 oz
whole hazelnuts will give 1 cup hazelnut
meal). To remove the skins from whole
hazelnuts roast in a 200°C (400°F) oven
for 5 minutes, wrap in a tea towel and
rub the hazelnuts vigorously.

## mascarpone cheese

A fresh Italian triple-cream curd-style
cheese. Its consistency is similar to thick
(double) cream and it is used in a similar
way. Available from speciality food stores,
supermarkets and many delicatessens.

## basic meringue mixture

**150ml (4¾ fl oz) egg whites**
**    (approximately 4)**
**1½ cups (225g/7⅞ oz) icing**
**    (confectioner's) sugar**
Place the egg whites in the bowl of an
electric mixer and beat until stiff peaks
form. Gradually add the sugar and beat
until the mixture is thick and glossy.

## puff pastry

Time-consuming to make. Available from
patisseries (order a block in advance) or
use the frozen supermarket variety, in
block form if possible, so you can roll it
out to the thickness you need. If using
store-bought sheets, you may need to
layer several to  the required thickness.

## rice paper

A translucent, edible paper made from
water and the pith of the rice-paper tree.
Flavourless, it can be used to wrap nougat
or line patty tins and eaten along with the
cakes or confectionery. Used traditionally
in Italian sweet cookery, especially when
making panforte. Rice paper is available
from speciality food stores.

## sponge cake

The basis for many instant desserts,
sponge cakes can be bought ready-made
from supermarkets or bakeries. You can
also make your own. If using the following
recipe for the lamingtons on page 40, you
will need to make two quantities. Use a
metal spoon when folding in dry ingredients
as metal cuts through the batter keeping
air bubbles intact.

## sponge cake recipe

**⅔ cup (100g/3½ oz) plain flour**
**¼ teaspoon baking powder**
**4 eggs**
**½ cup (110g/3¾ oz) caster**
**    (superfine) sugar**
**50g (1¾ oz) butter, melted**
Preheat the oven to 180°C (350°F). Sift
the flour and baking powder three times.
Set aside. Place the eggs and sugar in
the bowl of an electric mixer and beat for
8–10 minutes or until thick and pale and
tripled in volume. Sift the flour over the egg
and sugar mixture and gently fold through
using a metal spoon. Fold through melted
butter. Grease a 20cm (8 in) square tin
and line base with non-stick baking paper.
Pour the mixture into tin and bake for
25 minutes or until the cake is springy to
touch and comes away from the sides of
the tin. Cool on a wire rack. Serves 8–10.

### sponge finger biscuits

Sweet and light Italian finger-shaped biscuits, also known as savoiardi. Great for desserts such as tiramisu because they absorb other flavours and soften well but maintain their shape. These biscuits are available from delicatessens and most supermarkets.

### sugar

Extracted as crystals from the juice of the sugar cane plant or beet, sugar is a sweetener, flavour enhancer, bulking agent and preservative. It also makes ice-cream and custards smoother and helps keep cakes moist.

### brown sugar

Sugar that has been processed with molasses. It comes in differing shades of brown, according to the quantity of molasses added, which varies between countries. This also affects the taste of the sugar, and therefore the end product. The brown sugar referred to in this book is sometimes also called light brown sugar. For a richer taste you can substitute dark brown sugar.

### caster (superfine) sugar

Gives baked products a light texture and crumb, which is important for many cakes and light desserts such as meringues.

### icing (confectioner's) sugar

Is regular granulated sugar ground to a very fine powder. It often clumps together and needs to be pressed through a fine sieve before using. Always use pure icing confectioner's) sugar not an icing sugar mixture, which contains cornflour (cornstarch) and needs more liquid.

### regular granulated white sugar

Is used in baking when a light texture is not crucial to the outcome. Because the crystals are quite large, you need to beat, add liquids or heat regular sugar to dissolve it.

### sugar (candy) thermometer

A kitchen thermometer used to test the temperature of sugar syrup, jams and jellies during cooking. Marked according to the consistency of sugar syrup for sweet (candy) making. Available from speciality cookware and department stores.

### basic sweet dough

**2 teaspoons active dry yeast**
**5 tablespoons sugar**
**¾ cup (180ml/6 fl oz) lukewarm milk**
**2¼ cups (340g/12 oz) plain**
  **(all-purpose) flour**
**40g (1½ oz) butter, melted**
**1 egg yolk**

Place the yeast, 2 teaspoons of the sugar and all of the milk in a bowl and mix to combine. Set aside in a warm place for 5 minutes or until bubbles appear on the surface. Place the flour, butter, yolk and remaining sugar in a bowl. Add the yeast mixture and mix until a smooth dough forms. Knead on a lightly floured surface for 5 minutes or until smooth and elastic, adding a little extra flour to the dough if it becomes too sticky.

### tins

Aluminium (aluminum) tins are fine but stainless steel will last longer and won't warp or buckle. Measure tin widths at the open top, not at the base. If the tin has a lip, measure from the inside of the lip.

### bundt tins

Come in smooth and fluted versions. Whatever the shape, always grease the tin well. To remove a cake, loosen it with a palette knife and give it a slight twist.

### madeleine tins

Another speciality tin designed for just one recipe, but taste one of these little light-as-air cakes and you'll happily invest in one. Because of their delicate shell shape, madeleines do have a tendency to stick, so grease and flour the tins or spray with non-stick cooking spray.

### muffin tins

The standard sizes are a 12 hole tin, each hole with ½ cup (125ml/4 fl oz) capacity, or a 6 hole tin, each hole with 1 cup (250ml/8 fl oz) capacity. Great for making individual cakes and muffins. Non-stick tins make for easy removal, or line with paper patty cases.

### patty tins

These come in a variety of sizes but the standard is 2 tablespoon capacity. There are also shallow patty tins which are great for small tarts and pies. Grease the tins well before using or line them with paper patty cases for easy removal.

### round tins

The standard sizes for round tins are 18, 20, 22 and 24cm (7, 8, 8½ and 9½ in). The 20cm and 24cm (8 and 9½ in) round tins are the must-haves of the range.

### slice tins

The standard slice tin size is 20 x 30cm (8 x 12 in). These tins are great for slices or large slab cakes as well as roulades.

## springform tins

The standard sizes are 20, 23 and 24cm (8, 9 and 9½ in). The best tin to use for delicate cakes such as cheesecakes, mud cakes and layer cakes. The spring-loaded side collar lifts away, allowing for removal of the cake without the need to invert.

## square tins

The standard sizes for square tins are 18, 20, 22 and 24cm (7, 8, 8½ and 9½ in). If you have a recipe for a cake cooked in a round tin and you want to use a square tin, the general rule is to subtract 2cm (about 1 in) from the size of the tin.
So you would need a 20cm (8 in) square tin for a recipe calling for a 22cm (8½ in) round cake tin.

## tart tins

Are available in individual-serve to large sizes, may be deep or shallow, and come with or without removable bases. The standard sizes are 10, 20 and 24cm (4, 8 and 9½ in). Opt for the removable base for easy removal of delicate crusts, especially when using a larger tart tin.

## vanilla beans

These cured pods from the vanilla orchid are used whole, and often split and the tiny seeds scraped into the mixture, to infuse flavour into custard and cream-based recipes. If unavailable, substitute 1 vanilla bean with 1 teaspoon pure vanilla extract (a dark, thick, sticky liquid – not vanilla essence).

## vanilla extract

For a pure vanilla taste, use a good-quality vanilla extract, not an essence or imitation flavour, or use a vanilla bean.

# conversion chart

1 teaspoon = 5ml
1 Australian tablespoon = 20ml (4 teaspoons)
1 UK tablespoon = 15ml (3 teaspoons/½ fl oz)
1 cup = 250ml (8 fl oz)

# liquid conversions

| metric | imperial | cups |
| --- | --- | --- |
| 30ml | 1 fl oz | ⅛ cup |
| 60ml | 2 fl oz | ¼ cup |
| 80ml | 2½ fl oz | ⅓ cup |
| 125ml | 4 fl oz | ½ cup |
| 185ml | 6 fl oz | ¾ cup |
| 250ml | 8 fl oz | 1 cup |
| 375ml | 12 fl oz | 1½ cups |
| 500ml | 16 fl oz | 2 cups |
| 600ml | 20 fl oz | 2½ cups |
| 750ml | 24 fl oz | 3 cups |
| 1 litre | 32 fl oz | 4 cups |

# cup measures

| | | |
| --- | --- | --- |
| 1 cup almond meal | 110g | 3¾ oz |
| 1 cup breadcrumbs, fresh | 50g | 1¾ oz |
| 1 cup sugar, brown | 175g | 6 oz |
| 1 cup sugar, white | 220g | 7¾ oz |
| 1 cup caster (superfine) sugar | 220g | 7¾ oz |
| 1 cup icing (confectioner's) sugar | 150g | 5¼ oz |
| 1 cup plain (all-purpose) flour | 150g | 5¼ oz |
| 1 cup rice flour | 100g | 3½ oz |
| 1 cup cocoa powder | 120g | 3¾ oz |

If you love the great recipes in this book,
you'll love *donna hay magazine*

*donna hay magazine* features fresh, modern recipes
and styling ideas for every day and special occasions

special made simple

# donna hay
*magazine*

At the age of eight, Donna Hay put on an apron and never looked back. She completed formal training in home economics at technical college then moved to the world of magazine test kitchens and publishing where she established her trademark style of simple, smart and seasonal recipes all beautifully put together and photographed. It is food for every cook, every food lover, every day and every occasion. And, it is the style that turned her into an international food publishing phenomenon as a bestselling author, publisher of *donna hay magazine*, newspaper columnist, and creator of a homewares and food range.

books by Donna Hay: *off the shelf, modern classics book 1, modern classics book 2, the instant cook,* and *instant entertaining,* plus more.